Men are trash

The end of him and beginning of you

A collection of poems on break-ups, dating and healing.

Written by **FRANZISKA PUGH**

🐢Turtle Publishing

First printed in 2021.
Printed on demand in United States, Australia and United Kingdom.

Edited by Jane Turner from Write With Jane
Cover Design by Louise Vieillet Read
Interior Design by Kathy Shanks from Turtle Publishing

Published by Turtle Publishing

 **Turtle**Publishing

Contents

Always here for you girl

And you have boy problems, cause boys are problems

Introduction

This book has lived a lot of lives.

The story tried to die when it was just a little too hard to feel my feelings and remember what I was trying so hard to forget. This idea tried to flee when I couldn't open an old journal and face my pain. *Again.*

The momentum sparked with excitement after a glass of champagne when my newly-found fearless, independent-self felt good and joyous for the first time in a long time.

No matter what, it always stayed there
patiently waiting for the moments I felt ready again.

All I know after a decade of (un)successful dating,
a few moves across the world
and multiple cultural identity crises –
is that I'm still here.

This book is my attempt at owning my story.

Because when we own our journey,
we get to narrate the ending
and for now, that's all that matters.

What you will find as you read on is a narrative that roughly resembles a timeline of my journey into love —or rather— through love. I invite you to travel through these experiences with me as I learn what love is not, and maybe even ascend with me into a time of hopeful acceptance and compassion.

Stay soft,
Franziska

Pretty Girl Tax

I was named after my father's mistress.
What do you expect?

Designated Survivor

No matter how hard I've tried – and trust me – I've tried, life always pushes me to keep going.

It's like I'm drowning in the deepest ocean, getting stuck on the highest cliff, and suffocating in the smallest room.

And all of the sudden there's a window, a light, a space.

It's like, you can breathe a little easier, feel a little better, and step a little higher one day. Giving yourself grace in a moment of vulnerability, when you forget that you're supposed to feel only sadness and grief.

Suddenly everything feels ok.

Like a rock that skips over the water and slowly sinks into the depths as if it's greeting an old friend again after years of separation. When time and space meet after all that time apart, you were certain they'd forgotten how to find their way back to one another.

It's like the turbulence becomes a friendly wind on your face, and the tears show themselves less often because you've finally met your feelings where they were hiding in the depths of your body.

And then I become a little more grateful
for being the designated survivor.

Captive

It hurts to open my journals and read about the pain,
to be reminded of the moments that held me captive for so long.

What if I remember too much?

Raindrops

I see
and so it is

Book of Sunshine

A book of flowers and sunshine
isn't half as interesting
as a book of pain.

Valentine's Day

The first time I understood the need for a romantic relationship was in third grade.

The ball landed sweetly between us.

"Did you get a Valentine today?"
"No, did you?"

"No."

IO Years

At 10 years old
you should never have to worry about the weight
on your bones,
or the way your body looks in the mirror
that makes you look bigger anyway.

You should never have to feel embarrassed
about the way your hair falls on your shoulders
or why your dad didn't come home.

At 10 years old
you should never have to
change yourself for other people
instead of first learning who you are.

You should never have to navigate this world
on your own
waiting to be saved by someone
that would never come.

Damaged Goods

I only knew how to
give and receive
love the same way my parents did -

Forcefully.

Angels

Never quite figured out
why the stars were shaped like angels
why the ocean was so blue
why the way into a girls heart
always seemed so overdue

The One I Want to Forget the Most

My first love
was the most toxic one,
for it wasn't love at all.

We were two broken souls who found each other through love
notes, poetry and a need to be saved.

We allowed each other to drown, maybe because we hated each
other just a little more than ourselves.

My first love
was a karmic one,
for it shouted insecurities and pain.

We carved our initials into desks because we thought it would last
for all time, not understanding that what we actually meant was the
pain contained in our union that would become a prison bleeding
into our life and take years to break out of.

My first love, is the one I blamed myself for the most
but maybe because it was the one that hurt the most,
it was the one lesson I needed to learn.

Punishment

You made me believe
that I deserved to be punished.

I hung on to the pain
for so long
I actually believed it was true.

Salty

I'm always the salty one –
Never the sweet one that got spicy over time.

I'm always the psycho one –
Never the guarded one who cuts you off at first sign of danger.

I'm always the petty one –
Never the triggered one.

And even that wasn't enough
to protect me from heartbreak.

See Ya Later

I've never been good at saying good-bye,
I always said see you later.

Maybe that's why I can never let go.

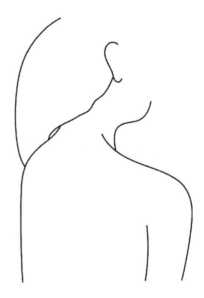

Oops

You hate me
for the same reasons
you love me.

A Gift

You told me that at 27
I wouldn't look at the world the same way
I was too optimistic, too naive, and too full of life
I believed in my goals and that got you excited
but my passions drove you away.

I made a point of accepting your challenge,
spending years being intentionally happy
and using your settling down to drive me forward
and show you that there's another way.

Now I'm 27,
and you're getting married on my birthday.

Think about me, too

What if I stopped thinking about you
and started thinking about myself

What if I stopped worrying about when you'd come back
and came home to myself

Downfall

We were the worst for each other,
and kept choosing each other anyway.

A Thousand Suns

You taste like
a thousand suns.

Devil

I'm glad I can laugh now
at the voodoo doll your sister made of me
and the fake numbers your mother would call me from
and the threatening phone calls from your dad
and the lies I believed
and most of all,
for thinking our experiences would make us stronger.

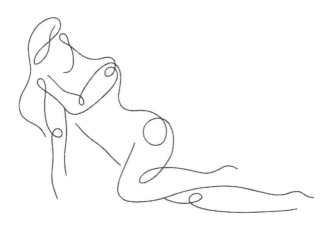

Peter Pan

What I can tell you about Los Angeles is that nobody wants to grow up. It's like a giant playground for adults who think they can live forever, and they'll die trying too.

Mostly sad, and a little funny are the overaged men who persuade women of something they never plan to fulfill. These men date so many women they forget their names and don't remember the last lie they told. They become so reckless in their endeavors that their carelessness is what keeps the women at bay.

On some nights, the skies are so clear you think you can fly away with them, believing their word will come to fruition one day.

We've done this dance before.
Nothing lasts forever.

Wait

"Don't wait for me."

FaceTime Lover

Back when we had that bi-coastal FaceTime kind of love,
the I-can't-wait-to-hold-you-again-type of love,
the type that made you call me at all hours of the night to
make sure you were the last one I spoke to before going to bed
kind of love.

Now the phone just rings
and nobody ever answers.

Handle with Care

Always too much
to handle
sort through
slipping into
and out of
worlds to expand
dipped toes
never wanting to be seen
always wanting to watch —

What a show.

Hate You Part I

I hate you for making me feel I don't deserve love
I hate you for making me feel insecure
I hate you for hating me
I hate you for comparing me to other girls
I hate you for lying to me
I hate you for making me feel like I'm the one that's crazy

Hate You Part II

The more I hate you,
The more I hate myself.

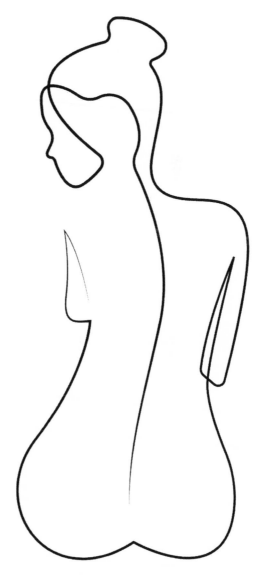

Liar

I'm a liar, too.

Advice I should take but don't listen to

- [ ] ~~Don't entertain fuckboys.~~
- [x] Allow time for self care. Every day.
- [ ] Let Go(d).
- [ ] ~~Don't eat everything on your plate if you're full (lll)~~
- [ ] "I'll remember this later" means you need to write it down ASAP.
- [x] Be your best friend first 🌼
- [ ] Drink more water if you're sad.
- [ ] ~~Don't~~ pop that zit
- [ ] Know that the comeback is always greater ♥

Games

You and I
became a game
of watching how far the other person would go.

Can't Come to the Phone

If only finding your phone hidden under the bathroom sink was the weirdest coincidence of them all.

Millions

Honey,
if he shows off how much money he has
he doesn't have any.

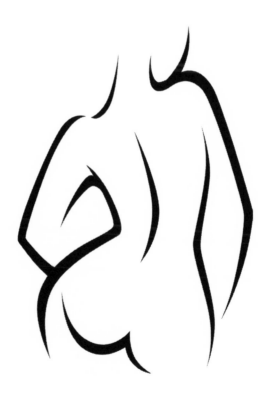

Overtime

You're staying late at work again
You used to stay late with me, too.

Finality

I feared the finality of writing this down
because that meant it was true.

We were never meant to be.

Poem With No Title

Girls with no story
are no fun
girls without a face
are never the ones
to light up a room
when everyone wants the
damaged one
to subdue

Can you handle her?

Trust Issues

It's not that I have trust issues,
It's that after a year of dating,
I get introduced as,

"The girl I'm seeing."

Intuition

I'm sorry for all the times
I thought I was at fault for the relationship ending.

For the instances I thought I was crazy
for arguing about my insecurities

When my
heightened emotions
high expectations
and control issues

weren't so unrealistic after all.

I was right all along
I'm always right.

Next life

Continue to pay for your ex's apartment
and tell me you don't buy girls flowers

See you never.

Redemption

Women are incapable of forgiving

Space

"I miss you. I just
wanted to give us
space because the
back and forth was too
intense. You're always
on my mind."

Forever and a Day

It took me forever and a day
where I didn't understand the way people showed me love
because I didn't love myself.

Assumptions

I always get in trouble
for misreading situations
after they occur.

I always hold on to
lifelines, no matter how small
they are
until they disappear.

And even then, I'll still throw a hook.

Sharkbait

The shadow of his presence still haunts me in small spaces, bathrooms where I feel someone is watching me and in public spaces where I keep a watchful eye on young girls. It's here I wait for men in sheep's clothing. Men like him.

It was a Saturday night and I was blissfully enjoying the loud music around us, fueled by the neon lights and change of colors in the water fountain. I was blissfully unaware of the dangers the world would show me, unaware of the trap my new friend would pose for me.

I just moved to the city I dreamt of my entire life. I wanted to start over and begin enjoying my life the way I always intended – bravely.

I used to blame myself for being young and naïve. There was even a time I felt proud of having gone through an experience, thinking bravery comes only from extreme situations. I know now that such a belief is as damaging as the situations that cause such thoughts.

I was warned about men like him. Sharks. I was told they'd promise me the world and then take everything from me. But I was different. He promised me a start in the music industry. I just needed to have a drink with him first.

The drink became more than I could handle, maybe because he continued to pressure me to drink more or maybe because he continued to move his body toward mine. When he followed me into the bathroom and convinced the girls I was too drunk to know what I'm saying, I ran.

I felt like a loser.

I was so afraid to speak out and stand up for myself. I was so afraid that my small stunt in the music industry was over because I wasn't "cool enough" to hang.

I'll never know what could have been, but I know that the stains from his recklessness will continue to bleed down Sunset Blvd.

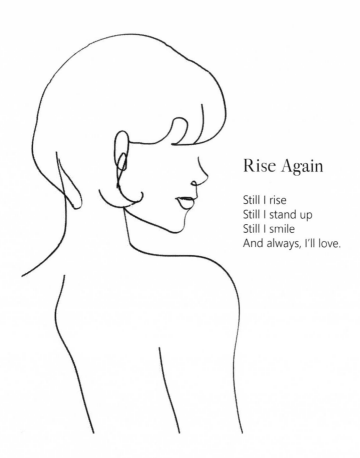

Rise Again

Still I rise
Still I stand up
Still I smile
And always, I'll love.

Dancing in the Moonlight

You took my hand
and spun me around
dancing after a night out.
The apartment was empty
and the sounds of laughter
bounced off the empty walls
echoing for neighbors.
Nobody seemed to mind,
nobody seemed to care.
We were free,

even if it only lasted that one night.

Pick-Up Lines & Tan Lines

I was so dumb,
I actually believed your
pick-up lines.

You

It was all about the chase
never love.

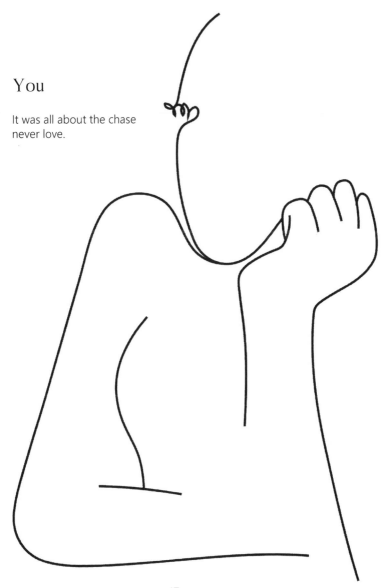

Someone Else

I thought he was afraid of commitment.
Turns out, he was committed the entire time.

A Modern Love Story

No seeds can grow
if nothing is planted.

Dear Diary

Today was a good day
I wish I wasn't too tired to tell you about it

Red Wine

I am at a bar with you. The world is shutting down tomorrow and you asked me to go on a date one last time before everything would change.

I forgot what it was like to laugh with someone else by my side. To make eye contact with someone across the bar, knowing I was yours.

Everything did change.

Heartbreak

By the time we learn to love again
we'll get our heart broken -
maybe that's what I'm scared of.

Sequoia

We played home
Without realizing what we were doing

Chasing others who didn't want us
To come together and take on the world

Maybe it was meant to be

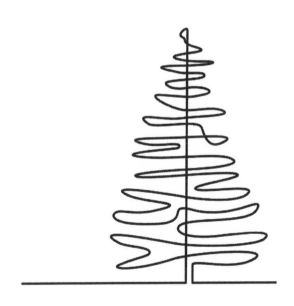

Made Me

God made me lose you
so I could finally learn to love myself,
befriend the woman I would become
and find the girl that went missing
all those years ago.

God made me grieve you
so I could find the depths of love
within me.

God made me forgive you
so I could forgive myself
for all the times I chose others over me.

Haven

If you wanted to,
you would have spoken
all the words you were
too scared to say

If you wanted to,
you would have walked away
from all the lies and deceit
to come home to me

If you wanted to,
you would have
built a safety
haven

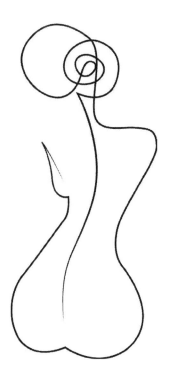

Perception

Every day you got a chance and a choice,
and every day you didn't choose me.

Guarded Woman

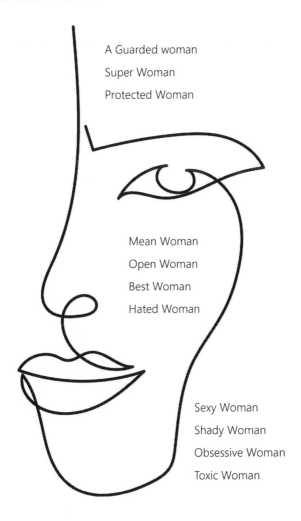

A Guarded woman

Super Woman

Protected Woman

Mean Woman

Open Woman

Best Woman

Hated Woman

Sexy Woman

Shady Woman

Obsessive Woman

Toxic Woman

Graveyard

You will become a graveyard
of all the thoughts you hoped
were your own,
of all the beliefs
your small world socialized you
to embody, and
all the people
you once thought
you were.

You will rise again,
too.

You will rise
to meet the person
you were meant to be,
change patterns you
were meant to break, and
take up space in this
infinite cosmos of chaos.

You will taste
the chance to start again.

Look back fondly
at all the memories and pain
because you know
that
to start again,
you have to allow yourself to die
too.

Works for Me

I'm just trying to
figure out what works for me
instead of
copying what works for everyone else.

Fairytale

Maybe I'll just stop one day
after all of this is over
and I've finally healed
this chapter

I keep holding on
for now
waiting for a chance
to change this story
just one more time

I made a life
creating fairytales for others
but always find myself alone

and this story isn't changing

Have to

It's a choice to hold on
and I don't want to let go

I thought we'd have more time
there's so much more to learn
and so much more to say

But I can't save you
not anymore.

Righteous

You were for real
but never for right.

I want to be

I always talk about who I want to be
when I grow up
never who I want to be with.

A Chase in the Desert

I never saw it rain
In the desert
Until a rainbow showed itself outside
Our door

I never believed roadrunners were real
Until we ran across the home
Like giddy children
Just to catch a glimpse

I never saw it snow
On the desert rocks
Until it melted on a fire
Inside our home

Succumbing to laughter and cherished sweetness

Until this too,
Came to an end.

A Pour

You can tell a lot about a man
by how much he pours for company

Pebble

It doesn't have to be
the red rose or the yellow sunflower,
It could be,
a cactus you found, or a
pebble you picked up on the driveway.

Just attention,
just a splash,
intention.

To speak
in our silence,
and show you care.

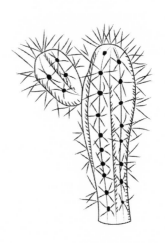

Some Days

Making the most out of your days
means making the least out of some, too.

Cold

It was a crisp day in the home we shared. The air was cold when it should have been warm and the breeze felt unfamiliar as I tiptoed to say my final goodbye.

It was obvious, then. It's always obvious.
This was the last time we would be together.

I picked up my last books, trying not to be too obvious in making sure I didn't forget anything.

Of course I forgot something.

It would only be a few weeks later when you came over to drop off the rest of my belongings. A few weeks is all it took for everything to change.

You gave me a kiss telling me everything would be alright.
It has always been too easy for you to lie.

The Afterward

What is an afterward
if it doesn't include you
Is there a happy ending for me after all?

What I Now Know

You were too pure for this world,
your beauty shone so bright,
others tried to dim your light to start their own.

My star,
my beautiful, innocent diamond,
your curiosity is your gift,
don't let others make you think otherwise.

My young babe,
I wish I could've prepared you for all the pain you will experience
but you're stubborn and want to learn through pain.

Remember,
we can't save everyone.
And yet, that's the one lesson I keep trying to learn.

Document OI

What do you
want to be remembered for?

Trenches

Now I'm out here thinking
all the guys are the same

Saw You Again

What would I tell you,
If I ever saw you again?

Women are trash,
too.

Sometimes

Just like the summer meets autumn
and walks bravely toward the cold
until it's greeted by spring,
so does the moon
welcome the sun
each day in a game of catch.

Just like the sun can shine a little brighter
and our laughs can sound a little louder,
so can we feel the breath in our bones
expand without knowing
growing into the familiar

So can I, love again

About the Author

Franziska is an author, media maven, brand architect and much more. She is a true visionary and celebrates womanhood and entrepreneurship by advocating for mindfulness and innovation.

Powerfully poised at the heart of global empowerment, Franziska is an incomparable impact leader and branding maven consistently positioning women for greatness in business and life. Crafting her own life's work around the transcendence of media and culture, Franziska's expertise as an industry trailblazer has propelled brands forward through the transformation of passion into purpose, helping each woman uniquely define and create success on their own terms.

When she's not channeling her inner Aries to generate creative chaos in every facet of her life, Franziska is creating healthy boundaries, scheming up ways to smash the Patriarchy, and living her best life in the city of Angels.

Photography by Anna Azarov

Made in the USA
Monee, IL
27 October 2021